Modern farm cidermaking. This view of an old ciderhouse at Tarrington, near Hereford, was taken in 1980. The semicircular arch behind the mill is an unusual feature – the ciderhouse is part of a barn which also contains two hop kilns.

CIDERMAKING

Michael B. Quinion

Shire Publications Ltd

CONTENTS

Published in 2008 by Shire Publications Ltd, Midland House, West Way, Botley, Oxford OX2 0PH, UK.

Printed in Great Britain by Ashford Colour Press Ltd, Unit 600, Fareham Reach, Fareham Road, Gosport, Hampshire PO13 0FW.

ACKNOWLEDGEMENTS
Illustrations are acknowledged as follows: Mr T. D. Brown, page 18 (bottom); H. P. Bulmer Ltd, pages 4 (both), 8 (both), 16, 18 (top), 31 (bottom left and right); Mrs E. M. Burge, page 23 (bottom); Mr Charles Evernden, page 22; H Weston & Sons Ltd, page 29 (bottom); Hereford and Worcester Libraries, page 23 (top), 24 (both); Hereford City Museums, page 3; Museum of Cider, pages 1, 2, 7 (both), 10, 11, 12 (bottom two), 13 (bottom), 14 (bottom), 17, 20 (top); Perry's Cider, page 31 (top); Michael B. Quinion, pages 6, 14 (top), 15, 20 (bottom), 26, 27, 28 (both), 30; R. J. Sheppy and Son, page 29; Taunton Cider Company Ltd, page 5.

The publishers acknowledge the assistance of Mr Giles Bulmer in preparing this reprint.

FRONT COVER: *A hand-operated cider press. Layers of apple pulp separated by cloths known as 'hairs', with their corners folded in to prevent the juice running away, were placed on the press and pressure was applied on the pile, called the 'cheese', until all the juice had been extracted.*

BELOW: *A typical costrel or firkin, with a horn mug. This costrel holds about half a gallon (2 litres).*

Herefordshire harvest workers taking a break. Note the communal costrel and single horn mug. By ancient custom, the horn would be filled and given to each man in turn, going clockwise round the cask.

INTRODUCTION

The countries producing cider today cover most of the temperate regions of the world, including Canada, the United States, Central and South America, Australia and many others. All of these have had the craft taken to them by emigrants from western Europe – Normandy, Brittany, Wiesbaden, the Basque country, Ireland and the western counties of Britain.

The farm cidermaking tradition of Britain mainly relates to the production of cider each autumn from fruit grown in the farm's own orchard, to be drunk by the farm labour force during the following year, especially the busy times of hay-making and harvest. Cider was not normally considered a cash crop, although farmers used to sell cider to local pubs, and cider merchants bought more for sale in the towns. It did not usually appear in the farm accounts and nothing was bought in from outside to make it, except the occasional cask. It was a private industry,

self-contained and unobtrusive.

Normally every labourer was given a daily allowance of cider, which was accepted as being part of the weekly wage, certainly as much so as the small piece of land to cultivate or the allowance of potatoes or firewood, or other perks that were given from time to time. The daily ration was about half a gallon (2-3 litres), served out from the big barrels in the farm cider house into individual small wooden bottles, made in the same way as casks. These were called *firkins* in the West Country and *costrels* or just wooden bottles in Herefordshire. Each labourer also had a drinking cup, holding less than a quarter of a pint (0.1 litre), made from a cow's horn.

A daily allowance of half a gallon seems a lot, but the men were doing a very strenuous day's work. Even so, the quantities of drink some of these labourers consumed were prodigious by today's standards. The little casks would probably be brought back at midday to be refilled if any task out of the ordinary were being done, whilst at haymaking or harvest cider was served in unlimited quantities. There are many reports of labourers regularly consuming 2 gallons (9 litres) a day at such times, and accidents were often caused by over-indulgence. There were frequent claims by temperance reformers in Victorian times that the intelligence of the labouring classes was being adversely affected by drink.

Cider was particularly important at harvest time because it was also the currency in which temporary workers were paid, together with bread and cheese. A farmer who did not make cider, or whose cider was undrinkable, found it more difficult to get the casual labour he needed and was reduced to buying good cider from someone with a surplus.

Because cidermaking was such a private craft, it is difficult to discover the amounts made each year. But it is possible to estimate production from the numbers of mills still to be found on farms, their size, the amounts of orchard in various counties and the quantities, for example, specified in auctioneers' sale notices. Taken together, these give a figure for Herefordshire production of some 1 to 3 million gallons (4 to 13 million litres) each year in the 1870s, and a total for Britain of anything from 5 to 15 million gallons (20 to 70 million litres).

Such a volume represents a craft of uncommon importance. It had as central a place in the farming year in the cidermaking counties as the harvest itself.

BELOW LEFT: *Lichen-covered branches of a heavily laden standard tree in an old orchard.*

BELOW RIGHT: *Tying a bud under the bark of a two-year-old rootstock in an orchard nursery.*

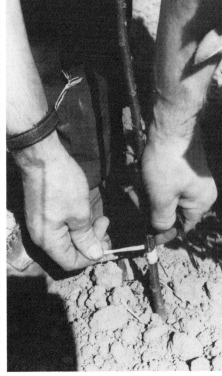

A modern Somerset bush orchard. These trees are planted at 240 to the acre, a much higher density than that possible with the old standard trees. Note the shortness of the trunks.

ORCHARDS AND ORCHARDING

Opinions differ about the right fruit to use for cidermaking. In the western and south-western counties of Britain makers believe that only special varieties, rich in tannins, make a cider worth the name. But in Norfolk, Suffolk, Kent and Sussex cider is regularly made from cooking apples like Bramleys and dessert fruit such as Worcesters, and local people seem satisfied with the blander tastes of such ciders.

Cider fruit consists of varieties more closely related to the wild crab apple than to eating or cooking apples. They are small fruit, hard, often heavily blotched and rather unattractive to look at. If you try to eat them you will immediately discover another unattractive feature – their high tannin content makes them taste bitter, and the juice dries the mouth, making the fruit difficult to swallow. The name for this is *astringency*.

But cider apples vary tremendously in the amount and type of tannins they con-

tain, as well as in their sugar and acid content. Pomologists (specialists in apple varieties) have divided cider apples into two main groups, bittersweets and bittersharps. As the names suggest, bittersharps have a higher acid content than bittersweets. Both have juice that is rich in sugar, which is the part that ferments to give alcohol. There are two other main classes of apple, sharps and sweets; both are low in tannins, the sharps being our cooking apples and the sweets the eating ones.

Traditionally, cider has usually been made from bittersharps – varieties like Foxwhelp, Cowarne Red, Dymock Red, Joeby Crab, Kingston Black and Skyrme's Kernel. Such fruit has always been supplemented with bittersweets such as Strawberry Norman, Knotted Kernel and Upright French, as well as with sweets like Eggleton Styre, sharps like Cider Lady's Finger and many others.

5

Using a hook pole to harvest fruit. This perry pear tree is 40 feet (12 m) tall, so a long pole is needed. The pears are small and hard and come down very fast.

Today the emphasis is more on bittersweets. The change has come about because of a slow evolution in public taste and in the way cidermakers use their fruit. Large makers often now use a mixture of cider fruit and culinary fruit like Bramleys, which increase the acidity of the juice. Using bittersweets gives the modern maker more flexibility in blending. Consumers now prefer their ciders smoother, less sharp and lower in astringency than they used to be, so that mild bittersweets are a better source of juice.

There are so many varieties of cider fruit that the whole of this book could be taken up merely with a list of them. Some of their names, like the Kingston Black or the Eggleton Styre, commemorate the places where they were first found or cultivated. Some recall their finders or popularisers,

like the Breakwell's Seedling or the Tom Putt, named for Sir Thomas Putt, an eighteenth-century Devon landowner. The Normans, and there are at least a dozen varieties with that word in their names, were so called because they were thought to have come from north-west France. Coccagee, a Somerset and North Devon variety, was brought over from Ireland in the eighteenth century (the name is said to mean 'goose turd' in Irish).

Today's bittersweets are almost all recent cultivars, and the modern cidermaker grows hardly any varieties known before 1900. But it is good to see strong names still being given to these modern apples – Brown Snout, Michelin, Dabinet, Yarlington Mill, Chisel Jersey – and not some anonymous number.

There are many other varieties, unnamed or known by some local name, to be found in small orchards all over the West Country – variations on a basic theme. The variation is due to the unfortunate habit of the apple not to breed true from seed. Old-time orchardists used to say that if you planted a thousand pips from one tree you would get a thousand different offspring and only two or three of them would be worth keeping.

Such *wilding* trees grown from seed were, therefore, useful only if a systematic attempt was being made to find new varieties. Once a grower had a tree he liked, he had to propagate it vegetatively by grafting or budding.

The two processes are similar but are carried out at different times of year. The older process is *grafting*. This involves taking a shoot from the parent tree when it is dormant in midwinter, keeping it cool and moist by burying it in soil until spring, and then inserting it under the bark of a young tree and binding it into place. The shoot fuses with the young tree but grows up with the characteristics of the parent. Wilding trees were commonly used as stocks on which to place the graft, as they were generally considered to have more vigour. In medieval times and later, the normal practice was to *head-graft* or *top-work* a number of shoots from the parent into slits in the sawn-off top of the trunk of a wilding that had been allowed to grow some 4 or 5 feet (1 m to 1.5 m) tall. Often as many as a dozen grafts would be made on

ABOVE: *Bagging the fruit to take it from the tumps in the orchard to the mill.*

BELOW: *By 1905, when this photograph was taken, a large proportion of the annual apple harvest was destined to be sold to the new cider factories. This orchard is probably at Credenhill, near Hereford, and the ton or so of fruit is being taken to Bulmers. There is enough fruit on the cart to make about 150 gallons (700 litres) of cider.*

7

ABOVE: *The present-day replacement for harvesting poles – this tractor-mounted tree-shaker is being demonstrated on a standard tree in a mature orchard.*

LEFT: *In bush orchards like these a blower is used to move the apples away from the trunks of the trees and then this gatherer collects them into a trailer (out of sight behind the tractor). It separates out the leaves, stones and other rubbish first.*

A Somerset apple tallet of the late nineteenth century.

one tree, not always from the same parent. Grafts have also been applied to young stocks near ground level.

A more modern technique is *budding,* which is done in midsummer by taking a bud from the parent and inserting it, again under the bark, into the base of a two-year-old rootstock within 6 inches (150 mm) of the ground. Virtually all apple trees nowadays are propagated in this way. Until very recently rootstocks grown from seed were usual, but much work has been done, particularly at the East Malling Research Station in Kent, to produce rootstocks with special properties, such as the ability to produce good crops early in life or to grow up as a dwarf tree.

Apple trees have traditionally been *standards,* growing some 20 to 30 feet (6-9 m) tall, with the main branches starting about 6 feet (1.8 m) from the ground. Though useful for old-style orchards, which served as protected winter grazing or windbreaks for the farmhouse, such trees are not very easy to harvest and take up a great deal of space. Hence dwarfing rootstocks are now usual. These produce trees only 6 to 15 feet (1.8-4.6 m) high, which can be grown so close-packed as to look more like a hedge than an orchard.

Such trees are efficient in their use of land and can be mechanically harvested, but the orchards are single-use and no longer give protection for farm animals.

The standard trees of old orchards were grown no closer than 30 feet (9 m) apart. When first planted, the orchard was often laid down to arable for the first ten years or so, until the trees were becoming mature and impeding cultivation (one of the other faults with standard trees is that they take a long time to start cropping fully, sometimes as long as fifteen years). Once at this stage, the land was turned over to grass. The typical crop from these orchards was low by today's standards, perhaps only 2 or 3 tons to the acre even in a good year. Today's bush orchards can give 10 tons per acre.

Because they are destined to be milled, the appearance of cider fruit is unimportant and so it has been usual to harvest them by knocking the fruit from the trees with poles. The poles were of ash, up to 15 feet (4.6 m) long, sometimes fitted with an iron hook to shake inaccessible branches. Fruit thus removed was gathered into piles. In the Herefordshire region the normal practice was to leave the fruit out in the orchard in heaps called *tumps,* covered with straw, for two or three weeks before milling. The idea was to allow the fruit to lose some of its moisture, to concentrate the sugars in the juice and to become mellow. Elsewhere, particularly in Somerset and Devon, the practice was to lay the fruit on the upper floor of the mill building or *pound house*. These floors were called *apple tallets*. Here the mellowing could take place without risk of damage from severe weather or of being eaten by animals.

When the fruit was judged ready, tested by the cidermaker being able to make a dent in its skin with his finger nail, the fruit was taken to the mill. Where tallets were used, it usually merely had to be shovelled into a chute leading to the mill below.

The making of perry from pears has been common in the western cidermaking areas for centuries. Perry is less well known than cider, but it has a distinctive flavour that makes it a prized drink among those who have access to it. The production of perry is very similar to that of cider, but perry pears ripen earlier than do cider apples and they do not keep at all, so it is usual to mill and press perry pears as soon as they have been harvested. The trees are a distinctive feature of the landscape in some areas, notably around the Herefordshire–Gloucestershire border, because they grow to be more than 50 feet (15 m) tall and often have an elegant curving top growth. They also live much longer than apple trees, and one can often find perry pear trees, still bearing plenty of fruit, of two hundred years of age. By this time an apple tree would be long dead.

One of the last circular stone mills in use in Herefordshire. This mill is on the Welsh border and the photograph was taken in the 1960s.

Using a stick to scrape 'must', or apple pulp, from the sides of a stone mill on the Welsh border of Herefordshire. The photograph was taken in 1978.

MILLING AND PRESSING

Because cider apples are hard, two steps are needed to extract the juice: first the fruit has to be crushed by some means, and then the pulp must be pressed to extract the juice.

In earliest times fruit was broken up by hand with a mortar and pestle or in wooden troughs. The first mechanical mill was similar to that used in other industries to crush rock or mineral ores. This was the circular horse-powered mill, in which one or more vertical grindstones were pulled around in a trough. Such mills were made from whatever suitable stone was available locally: in the Herefordshire region they were of a red sandstone conglomerate found in the Wye valley below Monmouth; in Cornwall and the Channel Islands they were usually of granite (and a more intractable stone to work into circular troughs can scarcely be imagined). Where

suitable stone did not exist, troughs and grindstones were made of wood, with the extra weight needed for effective grinding supplied by large stones laid on a platform across the axle of the grindstone.

The milling process was easy. A hundredweight (50 kg) or so of fruit was laid on the wooden or stone central pier of the mill and the horse was harnessed up. The cidermaker walked behind the horse, knocking a few apples into the bed of the mill as he went, using any old piece of stick that came to hand. After enough fruit had been crushed to cover the bed of the mill, a couple of buckets of water were thrown in. Milling then continued, with the cidermaker using his stick to scrape pulp off the sides of the mill and to nudge more fruit into the bed, until the wake in front of the grindstone threatened to throw pulp out on to the floor. By this time, the pulp was

11

ABOVE: *The original 'ingenio': a woodcut from John Worlidge's 'Vinetum Britannicum' of 1678.*

BELOW LEFT: *The Somerset version of the ingenio, drawn in 1886. Even at this time, most were still hand-operated.*

BELOW RIGHT: *During Victorian times the idea of the rotary mill was much developed. This large 'scratter' stands 5 feet (1.5 m) tall at the hopper. Note the large pulley for belt drive. Photographed in Worcestershire in 1971.*

deep brown in colour from oxidation and highly aromatic. The maker would test it by squeezing a little in the palm of his hand–if the squeezed pulp kept its shape when his hand opened, and the particles of pulp were all quite small, then it was ready to press.

Adding water during milling was an almost universal custom. It helped to prevent the part-crushed pulp from becoming too sticky and unmanageable in the mill and it seemed to lead to a quieter fermentation, with less tendency for the cider to go off. Adding water diluted the final product significantly, by about ten to fifteen per cent typically, but as farm cider, undiluted, could reach nine per cent alcohol in a very good year, some dilution was sensible, if only to reduce the rate of accidents during haymaking and harvest.

Milling one load of fruit, typically some three hundredweights (150 kg), took about half an hour, so the stone mill could scarcely be regarded as an efficient device. It also suffered from an insuperable disadvantage, which became a particular nuisance in Victorian times: it could not be mechanised. So cidermakers turned to a device that had been first described in the 1670s by John Worlidge, which it is said was based on the design of a Cuban sugar mill. This was the *ingenio,* a rotary crusher, consisting of a cylindrical toothed roller, whose teeth engaged with a fixed comb. Fruit dropping from a hopper above was chewed to pieces as it was forced through the comb by the teeth. Some later types were fitted with a pair of rotating wooden or stone rollers under the comb to complete the milling operation. These were geared to run in opposite directions at slightly different speeds and were often tapered to increase the shearing action.

This rotary or *scratter* mill was much quicker in operation than the circular stone mill, pulping several tons per hour without difficulty. But the rotary mill did not crush the fruit so finely as the old circular stone mills, and in particular the pips were not broken up. Some makers argued that they wanted the bitter flavour given to the juice by the aromatic oils in the pips. However, modern cidermakers go to great lengths to ensure that the pips are not crushed, and Bulmers, to take one example, at one time used waste pips from their mill to grow

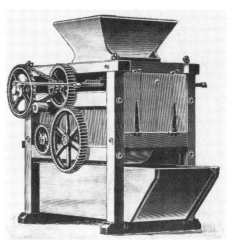

ABOVE: *The main suppliers of cidermaking equipment to the western counties (Herefordshire, Worcestershire, Shropshire, Gloucestershire and the Welsh borders) were Humphries of Pershore and Workmans of Slimbridge. This is Workmans' 1890 scratter mill. The crank on the rear chain-driven wheel operates a 'pusher' arrangement, which squashes fruit against the cutter periodically to improve the mashing of the fruit.*

BELOW: *A Gloucestershire woodscrew press, of unknown date but almost certainly eighteenth-century. The wood screw is 11 inches (280 mm) in diameter. Note the iron bands around the boss to prevent it splitting.*

ABOVE: *A typically massive West Country metal screw press, dating from the end of the eighteenth century. Note the windlass (left) to increase the force applied to the cheese. This press is now in the care of the National Trust at Cotehele House, Cornwall.*

LEFT: *This mid nineteenth-century twin-screw press is much less bulky than earlier types. Only the press bed is still substantial. This press has a particularly fine stone trough, set about 15 inches (380 mm) into the barn floor.*

A fine example of a Devon central-screw press. There is a ratchet mechanism on the upper press block to allow full pressure to be maintained on the cheese even though it is tucked away in a corner.

large numbers of wilding rootstocks for grafting.

Once the pulp had been milled, it was usually pressed at once, although a few makers practised another method, whereby the pulp was left to stand in open-ended casks for about twenty-four hours, which it was thought brought out more flavour.

Presses varied more in their design than mills. The oldest were made with a large central wooden screw, set into a massive headblock of oak, often weighing half a ton. The skill and labour required to turn these large screws must have been considerable. From about 1780 cast iron screws began to be made, first of all at Coalbrookdale in Shropshire, and then in other places. These cost five guineas from Coalbrookdale in the 1790s, a considerable sum. But they were so much easier to use and longer lasting that they quickly replaced the old wooden screws. Many presses from the eighteenth century show clear signs of having been converted when the wooden screw wore out or broke. Later still, from the 1830s onwards, a new design of press began to appear in which the heavy side supports for the headblock were replaced by two metal screws, with the headblock supported in collars held in grooves in the nuts used to screw the press down. These presses were much lighter than the older ones and led quickly to the establishing of the travelling cidermaker.

There are many regional variations in press design. In Somerset the characteristic type is a triple screw press, with the two outer screws worked by gearing off the centre screw. In Devon the wringing or pound house often contained a central screw design, the screw rising out of the middle of the press base, and having a press block operated by a ratchet mechanism.

This kind of press presupposes a method of pressing the pulp that allows it to be piled around the screw. Apple pulp itself is too wet and mushy to stay in place while being pressed, so the usual binder in both Devon and Somerset is barley straw. A layer of pulp is spread on the press bed, a layer of straw is put on top, followed by

15

Trimming the edges of the straw cheese with a hayknife.

another layer of pulp, and so on. This is then pressed. When all the juice that can be extracted has trickled out from the *cheese* or *mock* (the local names for the stack of pulp and straw), the pressure is taken off and the outermost layers of pulp and straw are cut off with a hayknife and piled on top. Pressure is again applied, and this process is repeated until no more juice can be wrung out.

In the Herefordshire region pulp has usually been contained in cloths, made originally of horsehair. A *hair* is laid on the press bed and filled with two or three buckets of pulp, and the corners of the hair are folded in. Another hair is then placed on top and the process repeated. With this method there is a risk that the pile of hairs will become unstable in the middle and slip out, creating an appalling mess and wasting much time and fruit. It looks very simple if you see an expert building a cheese, but it is far from easy. Some modern makers use a frame to ensure that all the hairs are made up to the same size, but this has traditionally been more usual

with the travelling cidermaker than with the farmhouse-based makers.

In eastern parts of Britain, notably Surrey, Sussex, Kent and Norfolk, makers have used yet another type of press, which has a box in place of the press bed. Pulp is put in the box, either with straw or by itself, and pressed. This style of pressing results from the use in these areas of culinary or non-cider fruit, the pulp from which is notoriously slippery and difficult to press using cloths or in unsupported straw cheeses.

The final stage in preparing for pressing is always to put a large, heavy board over the cheese to spread the weight and then to apply pressure, very gently at first. This is essential because the first touch of weight on the cheese causes a small flood, and if care is not taken a lot of juice can be wasted. Once the first flood is over, pressure can be applied more forcefully, and the cheese is soon reduced to about one third of its original height. It is usual to leave the press screwed down for some time, to allow the last few drops of juice to

Building the cheese in the Herefordshire style, using cloths or 'hairs'. Note the careful folding of the corners to ensure no pulp is lost.

ABOVE: *Pressing the cheese or 'mock'.*

BELOW: *Straw cheeses are still made, though the traditional long barley straw is now almost impossible to obtain. Ed Gifford is seen at work building a mock at East Pennard in Somerset in 1979. Note the frame to ensure a neat stack.*

18

come out slowly. These were prized, because the juice was sweet and clear and so very pleasant. But you drank more than a few drops at your peril, because it is strongly diuretic!

Once the last of the juice has been extracted, the pressure is taken off and the cheese dismantled. The dry pulp remaining is often called *pomace* and sometimes has been fed to stock. More usually it has been dumped under a convenient hedge, though care was needed to ensure farm animals did not get to it once it had begun to ferment, which it would do after a day or so. There are many stories of the effects that fermenting pulp has on farm animals, particularly chickens and pigs. Though the sight of a drunken chicken staggering around the farmyard is nothing other than ridiculous, an inebriated pig is quite a hazard and takes some dodging!

FERMENTATION

Usually the juice from the pressing was put straightaway into large wooden casks, holding between 60 and 120 gallons (270-550 litres), or sometimes into vats of between 200 and 500 gallons (900-2,300 litres), if the cider house served a large estate. Nothing was added to start the fermentation – traditional cidermaking knows nothing of yeast cultures – but the cask was carefully watched and kept topped up to the bunghole to prevent air getting into the juice and spoiling the cider. A brown froth would begin to gather at the bunghole after a few hours or days, depending on the temperature, and this would become white after a further interval. Both stages were watched with approval, indicating the juice was 'working'. Fermentation would take a week or two in warm weather but could take up to two months, or more, if the weather was cold. It was not uncommon for the casks to go silent for six weeks or longer in the coldest part of winter, only to start fermenting again in the warmer weather of early spring. Farmers preferred a slow fermentation because it gave a better product.

Farmers had no idea what caused the fermentation to take place and, as with other important matters involving unknowns, a rich folklore of methods and practices grew up around cidermaking. If a cask did not start fermenting fairly soon, a handful of earth was often poured in through the bunghole. Meat was often put into a 'sullen' cask, usually strips of bloody beef, but sometimes bacon, rabbit skins or other scraps. It was sometimes a farmer's habit to add barley or wheat to the juice.

Most of these customs have a basis in fact – meat adds essential nutrients to the yeasts, barley and wheat provide starch that can be converted to sugar and finally to alcohol. Even today, it is not known for certain where the yeasts come from that convert sugars to alcohol. For many years it was thought that they came in on the skins of the apples, but recent work has shown that this is not so. Perhaps the farmers had the truth of it when they added earth to slow-fermenting juice, and the yeasts are in the soil of the orchard.

Once the initial fermentation was over, the farmer would bung down the cask and seal the bung with lime cement, to keep out the air. For the next three months or so, a secondary fermentation would take place, caused by bacteria working on the tannins and some of the acids to create the characteristic mellow flavour of cider.

But this farm cider was a drink very different in character to that drunk today in British pubs. It was quite without sugar, because the methods normally used did not permit the fermentation to be stopped part way and all the sugar was fermented out to alcohol. It had a rich, tannin-derived flavour and was usually quite acid, because of the bittersharp fruit used in its making. Good farm cider had, and has, a unique quality, though not to everyone's taste. Much farm cider was poorly made and had often begun to go off by the time it was drunk. So the cider developed the reputation of being sour, sharp and strong, with a delayed effect like the kick of a mad horse – scrumpy, in fact. The usual description of such cider in Herefordshire is 'squeal-pig' cider, because that was the

ABOVE: *Pouring the expressed juice into its fermentation cask using a wooden bucket and 'tunpail' – a coopered wooden funnel. Wooden utensils are necessary because metals taint the cider and can be dissolved in sufficient quantities to make the drinker very sick. An eighteenth-century outbreak of 'colic', resulting in deaths, was traced to lead poisoning from the linings of presses. The disease was thereafter known as 'Devonshire colic'.*

BELOW: *Sign of a healthy fermentation: a froth of yeasts and impurities at the bunghole of a cask that is 'working'.*

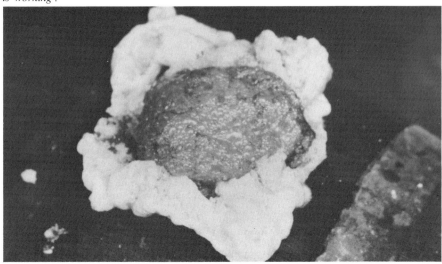

noise you tended to make on tasting it unawares. Another saying was 'the sort of cider that took two men to hold you while you drank it'. One very important quality it did have was its acidity. This helped it to keep and also meant that no disease-carrying germs could thrive in it. So it was, in general, always safe to drink, a useful characteristic in days when water supplies were often polluted.

During the making each autumn, one cask had special attention – the farmer's own. This was filled with juice from specially selected apples, free from any sign of rot and chosen from favourite trees. Often a new cask was used, one specially purchased from the local wine merchant or from the representative of a spirits importer. The best was one that had formerly held rum. It was most carefully *not* washed out. The cider took up the flavour of the rum from the wood, and the ullage added to the strength. This cask was broached on some special occasion or at Christmas the following year. At such times, the cider might well be served mulled – placed in a jug with spices like ginger and heated by plunging a hot poker into it.

Some makers practised special techniques designed to produce cider of a quality above average. These were time-consuming and so the prerogative of the larger mills on noble estates. Special care was taken at every stage – selected, sound fruit was used, the vessels were carefully scrubbed out and often fumigated with burning sulphur. The pulp was not pressed at once but left for about a day in an open-topped cask. It began to ferment and the cell walls broke down to release more juice and more flavour. The pressed juice would also be put into open-topped casks for a few days, with a little lime added. Another fermentation would throw up all the pectin substances from the juice, producing a thick brown crust. When this broke, the juice was siphoned into a cask and only permitted to ferment slowly. Periodically, the juice was *racked* into another cask, that is, the juice would be carefully taken off the deposit of yeasts at the bottom, the *lees*. The result was a cider that did not quite ferment out, leaving it naturally sweet and without any haze, because all the gelatinous substances had been removed. This whole process was called *keeving* and is very much the same as that used to make cider in France today, where the regulations do not permit any artificial sweeteners. The drink produced by these methods was highly prized and was bottled in earthenware containers to be taken to the gentry's London houses for the season, as a well regarded alternative to French wines. But it was very different from the rough, often hurriedly made cider that the farm labourers got.

THE TRAVELLING CIDERMAKER

The introduction of the rotary scratter mill and improvements in the design of presses led to an interesting development in Victorian times – travelling cidermakers. These seem to have been most common in the region of Herefordshire, Gloucestershire and the Welsh borders, though there are some fascinating references in Thomas Hardy's *The Woodlanders* that show such makers also existed in Dorset.

The cidermaker would be a local farmer or smallholder, although there are references to other trades in local directories and the like. Perhaps the most unusual were the undertakers, but the interest of such men in cidermaking was not purely because their employment in villages or small towns was by nature rather intermittent, but because they needed supplies of drink to serve at funeral breakfasts, and becoming a cidermaker was a not uncommon way of ensuring a cheap supply.

The maker would have a rotary mill, mounted on a low cart, with a twin-screw press, also on its own set of wheels. He would hitch these up one behind the other, ending the train with a flat-bed cart loaded with accessories like casks and hairs. This equipage would be towed from farm to farm by a team of horses, or later by a traction engine or even a tractor, for the travelling cidermaker continued to work

A travelling cidermaker at Goudhurst, Kent, using a traction engine as motive power. Note the characteristically small press of the eastern counties and, in spite of the risks of contamination, the tin dipper and galvanised buckets.

until well after the Second World War in some places.

On reaching their destination, the mill and press would be unhitched and placed at one side of the orchard or in the farmyard. If the cidermaker was using horses, a yoke would be fitted to the top of the mill so that the horse could power it by walking in a circular path around the mill, the power being transferred by means of a pair of bevel gears. Loading the apples into the hopper was then a matter of dodging the horse on your way in and out. Traction engines or tractors powered the mill by belting from a power take-off pulley.

Usually there would be a permanent team of two, the cidermaker and his assistant. The farm labour force was expected to do most of the work of moving fruit, juice, pomace and casks about.

Such travelling cidermakers were not so common in the main cidermaking regions but tended to do best around the edges, where comparatively small quantities of fruit were grown, or in places where the land was divided into smallholdings and farmers could not justify installing expensive milling and pressing equipment.

The travelling cidermaker had a very short season of operation, working in a set round from village to village and farm to farm, perhaps spending as long as two or three days at one place and then moving on. The work was charged at piece rates – around the turn of the century the usual price was a halfpenny or a penny per gallon. There is an illuminating document in the archives of the Welsh Folk Museum at St Fagans, Cardiff, that helps us to understand the work of these men. It is the account book of Mr C. T. Morris, who was a farmer near Raglan, but who took his mill and press to about forty farms between late October and mid December each year. In a typical season he would make between 11,000 and 18,000 gallons (50,000 to 80,000 litres) at an average price in the late 1920s of three farthings a gallon. This works out at some 350 gallons (1,600 litres) per farm, but it is clear from the

ABOVE: *A break in cidermaking in Gloucestershire in 1930. The pig has sneaked in to snaffle a little dropped pulp. The scratter mill is a particularly massive one, and the absence of the horse allows a good view of the 'horse works'.*

BELOW: *A travelling cidermaker in the yard of a public house at Ombersley in Worcestershire in the early years of the twentieth century.*

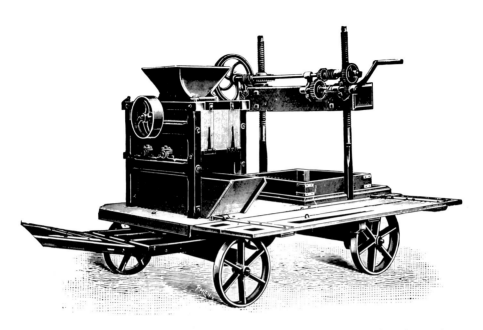

ABOVE: *The Workmans' combined kit for the well set-up travelling cidermaker, from their catalogue of 1904.*

OPPOSITE TOP: *Another Gloucestershire travelling cidermaker of the early twentieth century. In the background the horse (blurred by the long exposure needed at this period) is turning the mill. Note the two cheeses pressing, the one on the right fully screwed down, the other just beginning to press.*

OPPOSITE BOTTOM: *This portable press, like several illustrated, was made by a local agricultural engineer, and not by one of the two major manufacturers. The heart-shaped nameplate identifies it as being made by Alexander and Duncan, of Leominster. The picture dates from about 1930.*

records that many of the stops were communal sessions, so that the make for any one farm must often have been only one caskful, say 100 gallons (450 litres).

Mr Morris had no pubs on his round, but others often made at least one stop in an inn yard. Here, fruit bought by the landlord from local growers would be milled and pressed and the juice fermented in the cellars to supply customers' needs in the ensuing twelve months. Usually during these stops the fruit of the smaller orchardists of the whole village was milled, and the cidermaker might stay as long as a week.

For such makings, considerable care would be exercised in the work, but generally the travelling cidermaker's output was not so well thought of as that coming from the farmer who had his own mill and press. This may partly be put down to the natural prejudice of men who would always consider another cidermaker's output to be of lower standard than their own, but there was also some good reason for their view. The travelling cidermaker only came to a farm once each autumn, and so all the fruit had to be milled at one time, whether it was ready, overripe or still green. And a man working on piece rates might not always be fussy about picking out the rotten fruit or might not take much care over small details.

Stacks of fruit on the apple floor at H. Weston & Sons Ltd being carried to the mill by streams of water in channels. When new pressing techniques were introduced at Westons this method stopped being used.

Another 40 tons of fruit arriving in bulk at Bulmers' apple 'canals' in Autumn 1981. The stream of water flowing from the flume (left) serves the same purpose as at Westons. This silo has some 200 tons awaiting milling, enough to make 35,000 gallons of cider (160,000 litres).

FACTORY CIDERMAKING

Cidermaking went through a very bad period during Victorian times. The fine ciders produced by the keeving process were no longer made because French wines were more popular. Because of the agricultural depression orchards were neglected. Indeed, at one point in the 1890s it was seriously predicted that cidermaking would die out in Britain. That it did not is the result of a combination of circumstances. The work of Pasteur and others led to an increase of interest in and understanding of the processes of fermentation, and the new urban populations of South Wales, London and the West Midlands became ready markets for cider.

But it was not the traditional makers, the farmers and smallholders, who benefited from this new interest. They were unequipped by experience or inclination to exploit the new markets. Instead a whole group of small factory-based makers grew up in the cidermaking regions, buying fruit, making in bulk and selling to the cities. This was particularly marked in Herefordshire, because the coming of the railways had opened up this county, once more isolated than most, and because there were several large industrial city markets within easy reach, particularly South Wales and Birmingham. Between 1870 and 1900 no fewer than twelve factories opened around Hereford.

By presenting a source of cash for fruit, these new firms also contributed to the decline in farm-based cidermaking, for farmers tended to prefer to turn their fruit into a cash crop rather than, in effect, to give it away to their farm workers. Such payments of drink in lieu of part of the labourer's wages had, in any case, been rendered illegal when the Truck Acts were

This and the picture below show an industrial-scale development of the traditional cheese-building method that was still common at the larger firms in the early 1980s. It is now used only by some smaller makers.

LEFT: *Apples at Westons were pulped in a mill above and the pulp was released in pre-measured quantities down the chute. The cheese builders were using a frame (hidden under the polypropylene hairs) to keep the stack neat.*

BELOW: *Double-action hydraulic presses at Bulmers. While one press was squeezing out the juice (left centre) the cheese builders were making up another. These were replaced by continuous-action presses in the mid 1980s.*

The late Mr Richard Sheppy inspects his Swiss-made three-bed 'cloverleaf' hydraulic press in the ciderhouse at R. J. Sheppy and Son, Bradford-on-Tone, Somerset, in 1982. The three beds, which rotated about a vertical axis, allowed one cheese to be built or dismantled while the second was undergoing an initial press and the third a second one at a higher pressure. It has been replaced by an Austrian Voran belt press.

All the larger makers have now gone over to continuous presses, either hydraulic or belt types, which need few people to operate them. Tim Weston, the third generation of cidermakers at H. Weston & Sons Ltd, is standing by a hydraulic press installed in 2005 that can process 10 tonnes of apples an hour.

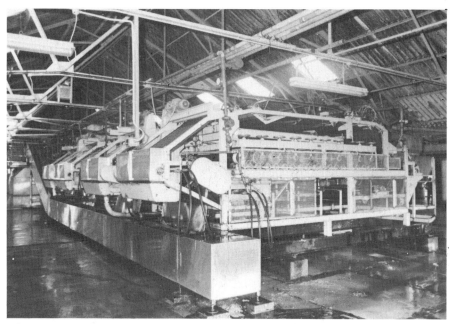

Bulmers introduced continuous pressing with these Swedish Ensink belt presses, seen in 1981. In belt presses, pulp is fed continuously onto a mesh belt and sealed by a converging belt from above; the belt and pulp 'sandwich' then passes between sets of rollers that apply progressively higher pressures to exact the juice. Note there's nobody about.

extended to agriculture in 1878, although, to judge from the evidence given to a Select Committee in 1908, this did not have much effect in some areas. The First World War interrupted the tradition, whilst increased education and wider horizons meant that the younger generation of workers preferred cash to cider, and the growth of mechanisation and other factors reduced the farm labour force to such an extent that making became unneccessary. In Devon and Somerset the tradition died rather realier than in Gloucestershire and Herefordshire, but by teh start of the Secpnd World War farm cidermaking was almost a thing of the past. Bt it has never quite died. Throughout the cidermaking regions of Britain there are still a few who make cider each autumn for their own consumption, and interest is growing once more.

With the great resurgence in interest in cider in the past quarter century, the best-known makers, such as Bulmers and Magners, have consolidated their position. They use sophisticated methods and have, for example, abandoned the labour-intensive building of cheeses in favour of presses that run continuously without moment-by-moment attention. Over the same period many smaller makers have enlarged their operations to supply supermarkets and pubs and more makers have come into the business to meet the growing interest in speciality and craft ciders. A century of development and research has led to company cidermakers being able to make a stable, sweet product, with or without carbon dioxide to add sparkle, in a wide range of blends, each with its characteristic flavour.

Automatic bottling lines that produce ten or twelve thousand litre bottles of cider every hour are along way from the patient horse and primitive equipment of a century ago. But the tradition is a continuous one and full of vigour.

LEFT: *Typical of fermentation and storage vats at medium-sized makers, these stainless steel vessels are at Perry's Cider, Dowlish Wake, Somerset. Each contains 1200 gallons (5500 litres).*

BELOW: *Their replacements, though reflecting growth in the business and requiring much less maintenance, lack the craft feel of older storage methods. These three tanks, the biggest holding 160,000 gallons (720,000 litres) are among more than 50 in Bulmers tank farm, a local landmark in Hereford.*

LEFT: *Though wooden storage vats are still in use at some makers, the larger ones have abandoned them because of their high maintenance costs. These are three of the 121 storage vats that Bulmers once used for storage. Each was 30ft (9 metres) high and contained 60,000 gallons (270,000 litres). All have now been dismantled.*

FURTHER READING

Campaign for Real Ale. *CAMRA Good Cider Guide*. 2005.
Copas, Liz. *A Somerset Pomona: The Cider Apples of Somerset*. Dovecote Press, 2001.
Crowden, James. *Cider: The Forgotten Miracle*. Cyder Press Two, 1999.
Juniper, Barri Edward & Mabberley, David J. *The Story of the Apple*. Timber Press, 2006.
Pooley, Michael J. & Lomax, John. *Real Cider Making on a Small Scale*. Special Interest Model Books, 1999.
Proulx, Annie & Nichols, Lew. *Cider: Making, Using and Enjoying Sweet and Hard Cider*. Storey Books, US, paperback, 2003.
Quinion, Michael. *A Drink for its Time*. Published by and obtainable from the Museum of Cider. (see below).
Watson, Ben. *Cider, Hard and Sweet*. Countryman Press, 1999.

Some others, out of print, that may be worth searching out:
Correnty, Paul. *The Art of Cidermaking*. Brewers Publications, US, 1995.
French, Dr R. K. *The History and Virtues of Cyder*. Robert Hale, 1982.
Legg, Philippa. *Cidermaking in Somerset*. Somerset Rural Life Museum, 1984)
Mac, Fiona. *Ciderlore: Cider in the Three Counties*. Logaston Press, 2003.
Orton, Vrest. *The American Cider Book*. Farrar, Strauss and Giroux, New York, 1973.
Williams-Davies, John. *Cider Making in Wales*. Welsh Folk Museum, 1984

PLACES TO VISIT

The Cider Museum, 21 Ryelands Street, Hereford, HR4 OLW. Telephone: 01432 354207. Website: www.cidermuseum.co.uk

Cornish Cyder Farm, Penhallow, Truro, Cornwall, TR4 9LW. Telephone: 01872 573356. Website: www.thecornishcyderfarm.co.uk

H Weston & Sons Ltd, The Bounds, Much Marcle, Herefordshire, HR8 2NQ. Telephone: 01531 660233. Website: www.westons-cider.co.uk

Hecks Farmhouse Cider, 9-11 Middle Leigh, Street, Somerset, BA16 OLB. Telephone: 01458 442367. Website: www.hecksfarmhousecider.co.uk

Mill House Cider Museum, Owermoigne, Nr. Dorchester, Dorset, DT2 8HZ. Telephone: 01305 852220. Website: www.millhousecider.co.uk

Perry's Cider Mills, Dowlish Wake, Ilminster, Somerset, TA19 ONY. Telephone: 01460 55915. Website: www.perryscider.co.uk

Rich's Farmhouse Cider, Mill Farm, Watchfield, Highbridge, Somerset, TA9 4RD. Telephone: 01278 783651. Website: www.richscider.co.uk

Sheppy's Cider Limited, Three Bridges, Bradford-on-Tone, Taunton, Somerset, TA4 1ER. Telephone: 01823 461233. Website: www.sheppyscider.com

Somerset Rural Life Museum, Abbey Farm, Chilkwell Street, Glastonbury, Somerset, BA6 8DB. Telephone: 01458 831197. Website: www.somerset.gov.uk/museums

Thatchers Cider Company Ltd, Myrtle Farm, Sandford, Somerset, BS25 5RA. Telephone: 01934 822862. Website: www.thatcherscider.co.uk

WEBSITES
In addition to the site-specific websites listed above, some others are:
Cider and Perry Trail: www.malverntrail.co.uk/cider.htm
Herefordshire Cider Route: www.ciderroute.co.uk Lists local attractions and includees two cycle trails.
Real Cider and Perry: www.ciderandperry.co.uk Includes a searchable list of UK producers.